DISTINCT FEATURES:

From Africa to South Carolina

By

Shiela Martina Keaise

MsLiteracy.com

This book is dedicated to people who live in the service of others, especially to my Aunt Elflorence Oliver, who serves without acknowledgement or appreciation!

Martina Publishing, Inc., PO Box 1216, Walterboro, SC 29488
www.MsLiteracy.com

DISTINCT FEATURES: From Africa to South Carolina.
By Shiela Martina Keaise.

SUMMARY:
This creative biographical picture book highlights the lives of African Americans in South Carolina and observes their lives. It sheds light on twelve African descendants who came to South Carolina with distinct features of Big Eyes, Wide Noses, Full Lips, and Large Ears.
These Distinct Features allow readers to see the characteristics behind the known physical features of life-changing Americans of African descent. This book uses eyes, nose, lips, and ears to describe the characteristics of these African Americans as they help themselves and other. Television theme songs of the 1960s, 1970s, 1980s, and 1990s capture their life's work as the lyrics tell their story.

Author's Note:
South Carolina is abbreviated SC and television is abbreviated TV throughout the book. Pictures are taken from Wikipedia and personal collection and are free to public. TV Theme Songs are used because of the author's love of music and the lyrics are descriptive and based on the lives of those depicted in this book.

Target Audience: Ages 7 – 12

ISBN: 978-0-9998665-5-9
Library of Congress Control Number: 2024907489

[1. Biographies—South Carolinians. 2. African Americans— Juvenile Literature. 3. Characteristics—Nonfiction. 4. TV Theme Songs—Television Themes. I. Title]

Cover design by: Michelle Strickland and Md Nazmul islam

Table of Contents

They say Africa is the motherland of all civilizations! Before there was America, there was Africa. Their lands were prosperous, their crops were bountiful, and their trees were fruitful.

Africans are people of strength, courage, and determination. They say Africans are born with distinct features. You might have heard of them.

Big Eyes, Wide Nose, Full Lips & Large Ears.

After researching the lives of 12 African descendants who came to South Carolina (SC), I found that these distinct features still exist. I discovered what these African Americans' well-defined features meant.

They used their *Big Eyes to envision a brighter day.*

They used their *Wide Noses to smell the fragrance of the arts.*

They used their *Full Lips to speak and spread the truth.*

They used their *Large Ears to listen to people's needs and concerns.*

Robert Smalls

Born in Beaufort, SC, Robert Smalls was the first "Greatest American Hero" of the Civil War.

Robert Smalls used his *Eyes to envision freedom from slavery*. He proved to be a trusted enslaved person, and when he had the opportunity, he used his status to free himself and sixteen others from slavery by impersonating the Captain of the Planter. He sailed a Confederate ship to freedom in 1862.

Robert Smalls used his *Nose to smell the fragrance of Politics*. He served as Captain of the USS Planter for the Union Army during the Civil War and fought in 17 battles. He later became one of SC's most respected US Congressmen. He served five terms in the House of Representatives between 1875 - 1887.

Robert Smalls used his *Lips to speak up for and defend children by introducing legislation that protected their rights*.

Robert Smalls used his *Ears to hear the cries of African Americans for education*. He lobbied for public education to be a key component of the new document. He believed that all they need is an equal chance in the battle of life.

Augusta Baker

Although she was not a native of SC, Augusta Baker made her mark in Columbia, SC, by being honored as America's First Lady of Traditional Storytelling. She told the "Facts of Life" in her stories.

Augusta Baker used her *Eyes to envision a collection of African American books accurately portraying black children and their culture.* Her collection opened the door for the Coretta Scott King Book Award given to AfricanAmerican authors and illustrators who best portray black life.

Augusta Baker used her *Nose to smell the fragrance of Storytelling and Literature.* She had a gift to dramatize stories without using puppets or props. Her love of the art of literature led her to become a leading authority on children's literature.

Augusta Baker used her *Lips to speak the "Facts of Life" through her stories.* She lit a candle and told a story.

Augusta Baker used her *Ears to hear the University of SC in Columbia's desire to have a Storyteller-in-residence.* Her decision to serve in this job for over a decade led to the creation of the annual Augusta Baker's Dozen Storytelling Festival in her honor.

Earl Matthew Middleton

Earl Matthew Middleton is a son of SC in many ways. He was born in Orangeburg, SC. He graduated from Claflin College, now Claflin University in SC. He completed 65 hours of training in an all-black pilot squadron in SC. He built and ended his career with "Cheers" in SC.

Earl Matthew Middleton used his *Eyes to envision himself as a successful entrepreneur.* He opened a barber's shop, and then a real estate company called Caldwell Bankers and started an insurance agency called Middleton Agency.

Earl Matthew Middleton used his *Nose to smell the fragrance of Socialization.* He loved people and looked beyond racial boundaries by employing whites and blacks.

Earl Matthew Middleton used his *Lips to encourage young people to work hard and have determination.* I was fortunate to have interned with Mr. Middleton during my college years, and he gave me common-sense advice. He also demonstrated his love of people by the way he treated everyone he met.

Earl Matthew Middleton used his *Ears to hear the cries of his community by becoming an active political leader in both the Republican and Democratic parties.* His commitment led him to become the head of the largest real estate agency in Orangeburg, SC.

Mary McLeod Bethune

Born in Mayesvilles, SC, to parents freed from slavery after the Civil War, Mary McLeod Bethune earned her name as an educator and friend—a true "Golden Girl."

Mary McLeod Bethune used her *Eyes to envision a school for Negro children by starting what would later become Bethune-Cookman College.* She devoted her life to ensure the right to education and freedom from discrimination for African Americans.

Mary McLeod Bethune used her *Nose to smell the fragrance of Education.* She graduated from the Moody Bible Institute in Chicago and taught at the Kindress Institute near Sumter, SC.

Mary McLeod Bethune used her *Lips to advise US presidents on racial affairs and the needs of African Americans.* She spoke up and as a civil rights pioneer and became the first African American to represent a state in Statuary Hall.

Mary McLeod Bethune used her *Ears to hear the injustices and complaints of African American women by founding the National Council of Negro Women.* She was a successful organizer, fundraiser, and a political activist.

James E. Clyburn

A native of Sumter and current residence of Columbia, SC, James E. Clyburn is a well respected Congressman on the "Law Boat" and highest ranking African American in Congress today.

James E. Clyburn used his *Eyes to envision laws that would change the country and state of SC for the educational good by supporting and creating legislation that builds schools and libraries.*

James E. Clyburn used his *Nose to smell the fragrance of politics.* His skill in this art caused his peers to elect him Majority Whip—the third ranking leadership position in the US House of Representative between 2007 and 2011 and between 2019 and 2023.

James E. Clyburn used his *Lips to educate youths by serving as a teacher and director of the community development project in Charleston, SC.* He continuously sought new and additional funding for education. for special education, a lower interest rates on federal student loans, and voted for improvements in Pell Grant funding for college loans.

James E. Clyburn used his *Ears to hear the concerns of the people by serving on the Veteran Affairs and the Transportation and Infrastructure Committees to name of few.*

Elflorence Oliver

Although not born in SC, Elflorence Oliver spent most of her life in Dorchester and Walterboro, SC. Affectionately known as Aunty by her nieces and nephews, her influence spread across the country through the lives of those she served and advised, just as Alice did on “The Brady Bunch.”

Elflorence Oliver used her *Eyes to envision the educational and spiritual success of her siblings and her nieces and nephews.* She encouraged and prepared her loved ones (including me) to attend college and live godly through strong discipline and truth.

Elflorence Oliver used her *Nose to smell the fragrance of self-respect and self-discipline.* By teaching all who would listen, she unselfishly showed that we need the self-duo of respect and discipline to go very far.

Elflorence Oliver used her *Lips to speak the truth about the wrong things she saw that needed to be corrected.* She never accepted bribery because she said it would silence you. Her lips spoke about my success in my future and now I get to write about it.

Elflorence Oliver used her *Ears to hear the cries of those doomed for failure.* As a result, she fed, corrected, advised, loved, and directed us in the things of God by a committed, selfless life she wanted us to follow.

Nelson B. Rivers III

Nelson B. Rivers III is a community leader determined to improve things for his community in Charleston, SC. As an ordained Baptist preacher, husband, and father of four, He realizes that "Family Matters."

Nelson B. Rivers III used his *Eyes to envision the importance of an organization that would improve the lives of young and old by serving over 30 years as a leader of the NAACP.* He has risen throughout the ranks of the NAACP to become the Chief Operating Officer of the oldest and most revered civil rights organization.

Nelson B. Rivers III used his *Nose to smell the fragrance of Oration.* With his oratory skills, he has used his professionalism to inform the community through humor with known facts. I am fortunate to have heard many speeches that he has given.

Nelson B. Rivers III used his *Lips to preach good news to all that would hear.* He served as Pastor of the Charity Missionary Baptist Church in North Charleston, SC.

Nelson B. Rivers III used his *Ears to hear the cries of his community by encouraging people in the local, state, and national arenas by energizing and enlightening them to change for the good.*

Marquetta L. Goodwine

Queen Quet, Chieftess of the Gullah/Geechee Nation, was born Marquetta L. Goodwine. She proved that working with state, national, and international leaders can make the dreams of the Gullah/Geechee people come true. Like the theme song of "Laverne and Shirley," Queen Quet, a native of St. Helena Island, SC, did it her way.

Queen Quet used her *Eyes to envision the Gullah/Geechee Sea Island Coalition, which aims to protect the environment and ensure these diverse people engage in the outdoors and the policies governing them.*

Queen Quet used her *Nose to smell the need to advance the idea of keeping the Gullah/Geechee culture alive.* Because of her leadership and dedication, Queen Quet worked with US Congressman James Clyburn to get "the Gullah/Geechee Cultural Heritage Act" passed or enacted.

Queen Quet used her *Lips to educate the public by speaking at the United Nations, national conferences, schools, and libraries, sharing facts about the Gullah culture.* I was privileged to have Queen Quet visit our library for twenty years.

Queen Quet used her *Ears to hear the cries of the Gullahs and Geechees to become recognized as one people.*

Cecil J. Williams

Cecil J. Williams is known to the world as the photographer from Orangeburg, SC, who chronicled the Civil Rights Era. He showed "A Different World" through his photographs of students at Claflin University, President Kennedy, Thurgood Marshall, and other civil rights leaders.

Cecil J. Williams used his *Eyes to envision the dreams of freedom and justice during the Civil Rights Era by taking pictures that captured their hopes and fears.*

Cecil J. Williams used his *Nose to smell the fragrance of photography.* At the age of 15, he began working as a professional and freelance photographer.

Cecil J. Williams used his *Lips to speak through the images that he captured and published in 126 books, 17 newspapers, 11 television documentaries and in the three books he wrote.*

Cecil J. Williams used his *Ears to hear the desire of Claflin University, South Carolina State University and the SC NAACP to capture the ultimate college experience by serving as official yearbook photographer.*

Kimberly Clarice Aiken

Before a cheering audience in Atlantic City, NJ, Kimberly Clarice Aiken was the first African American from SC to win the crown of Miss America. At 19, she suddenly climbed to the top just like "The Jeffersons."

Kimberly Clarice Aiken used her *Eyes to envision an organization providing aid to the homeless.* She founded HERO—Homeless Education and Resource Organization to provide necessary resources, support, and referrals to help homeless children and youth succeed and have a positive school experience.

Kimberly Clarice Aiken used her *Nose to smell the fragrance of pageantry.* She received training in voice, drama, modeling, and dance. Her talent, poise, and intellectual ability charmed the nation and prepared her for the coveted crown in 1993. She wore the crown with dignity.

Kimberly Clarice Aiken used her *Lips to entertain and inspire audiences with motivational speeches using her varied experiences.* She shared stories of her overcoming obstacles like brain surgery.

Kimberly Clarice Aiken used her *Ears to hear the cries of the homeless by encouraging her peers to volunteer to help in homeless programs.* At just 14 years old, she had a concern and read to children who stayed in shelters.

James Brown

James Brown is a legend! He is known as the Godfather of Soul and was born in Barnwell, SC. Through his music, he said, "Gimme A Break!" That break came when talent scout Ralph Bass heard Mr. Brown sing on the local radio and was so impressed with the fire in James Brown's performance that he immediately signed the group to King Records.

James Brown used his *Eyes to envision his dream of becoming a successful entertainer.* He educated himself in music by recording 75 top 20 hits (17 of which reached #1).

James Brown used his *Nose to smell the fragrance of dancing and singing by creating dance moves that other famous singers and groups have followed.* Michael Jackson was one of the singers who studied his moves to perfection.

James Brown used his L*ips to speak out against racism, sexism, and the need for improved education.* He proved to be one of the most important civil rights activists of the 1960s and 1970s.

James Brown used his E*ars to hear the concerns of the times and created sounds that appealed to Blacks and Whites.* His music broke the boundaries of racial segregation of the 1950s.

Jesse Jackson

Jesse Jackson is a political genius. Although he is known for being the first African American to make the highest bid for the top office in the United States, most do not know that Mr. Jackson was born in Greenville, SC. By his consistent character and strength, Mr. Jackson proved that "Green Acres" is the place to be.

Jesse Jackson used his *Eyes to envision his dream of becoming the first African American President of the United States of America.* He became a candidate for the Democratic presidential nomination in 1984 and 1988.

Jesse Jackson used his *Nose to smell the fragrance of equality.* By championing himself as a civil rights leader, he participated in several marches and protests against injustice, worked with Martin Luther King Jr., and advised presidents to eradicate injustice.

Jesse Jackson used his *Lips to speak out against injustice wherever it lurked.* During the 1980s and 1990s, he was the leading voice in the African American community and on an international level for opening new doors to Wall Street. He negotiated the release of US soldiers and civilians around the world in Syria (1984), Iraq (1990), & Yugoslavia (1999).

Jesse Jackson used his *Ears to hear the concerns of the people by establishing Rainbow/PUSH (People United to Save Humanity).* The organizations pursue social justice, civil rights, and political activism.

These are just a few African Americans from South Carolina with these distinct features. They are also characteristics that I adopt on a daily basis:

Big Eyes to envision a brighter day.

Wide Nose to smell the fragrance of the arts.

Full Lips to speak and spread the truth.

Large Ears to hear people's needs and concerns.

I am an African American from South Carolina and it is an honor to share some of the distinct features in role models used in this book that inspire me to serve my community.

TV THEME SONGS

Scan and listen to the lyrics of each TV Theme Song, which represent the lives of the 12 African Americans in this book. According to Rolling Stone, some are among the 100 Greatest TV Theme Songs of All Time in the "Scan Me" above.

'The Greatest American Hero'
ABC, 1981-1983

#29 Greatest TV Theme Song

'Facts of Life'
NBC, 1979-1988

< Second Season here

'Cheers'
NBC, 1982-1993

#13 Greatest TV Theme Song

'The Golden Girls'
NBC, 1985-1992

#38 Greatest TV Theme Song

'The Love Boat'
ABC, 1977-1986

#48 Greatest TV Theme Song

'The Brady Bunch'
ABC, 1969-1974

#2 Greatest TV Theme Song

'Family Matters'
CBS, 1989-1998

One Season here >

'Laverne & Shirley'
ABC, 1976-1983

#36 Greatest TV Theme Song

'A Different World'
NBC, 1987-1993

Three Seasons here >

'The Jeffersons'
CBS, 1975-1985

#1 Greatest TV Theme Song

'Gimme a Break'
NBC, 1981-1987

< Two Seasons here

'Green Acres'
CBS, 1965-1971

#80 Greatest TV Theme Song

About the Authors

Shiela Martina is the author of children's and adult books. She retired after 28 years of as a Children's Librarian and is now the Executive Director of the nonprofit, Community Innovation, she founded.
In Shiela's free time, she enjoys singing, editing, training, mentoring, and publishing books for new authors. When she is not doing all of those things, she enjoys taking care of her Aunt's goats, chickens, and cats Bashful and Zee.

Made in the USA
Columbia, SC
16 July 2024